being a
snowboarder

Cindy Kleh

Lerner Publications Company
Minneapolis

First American edition published in 2013 by Lerner Publishing Group, Inc.
Published by arrangement with Wayland, a division of Hachette Children's Books

Lerner Publications Company
A division of Lerner Publishing Group, Inc.
241 First Avenue North
Minneapolis, MN U.S.A.

Website address: www.lernerbooks.com

Library of Congress
Cataloging-in-Publication Data

Kleh, Cindy.
    Being a snowboarder / by Cindy Kleh.
       p.   cm. — (On the radar: awesome jobs)
    Includes index.
    ISBN 978–0–7613–7780–1 (lib. bdg. : alk. paper)
    1. Snowboarding. I. Title.
GV857.S57K54 2013
796.939—dc23   2011052664

Manufactured in the United States of America
– CG – 7/15/12

Acknowledgments: Bomber Industries 14bl; Jeff Brockmeyer 22l, 22c; Dreamstime: Millaus 12l, Monner 2t, 16–17, Francesco Vaninetti 12b; Mark Fox 18l; Getty Images: Johannes Kroemer 8, Doug Pensinger 9, Paul Krahulec 18-19, 19r; Nora Miller 23; O'Neill 22b, 22r; Shutterstock: Action Photos 28r, Ayazad 27, Brian Finestone 29br, Caleb Foster 21r, Ben Haslam 4tl, Ben Heys 10–11, Blazej Maksym 29l, Ilja Masik 2c, 30-31, 19bl, Mountainpix 3tl, 4–5, Norbert A 20r, Maxim Petrichuk 12 Samot cover, Strider 29tr, Kaleb Timberlake 20l, Tkemot 3br, Ventura 1, 15br, 24–25, Wildnerdpix 21l; SixSixOne Protection (One Industries, Inc.) 14tr, 15tr.

Main body text set in Helvetica Neue LT Std 13/15.5.
Typeface provided by Adobe Systems.

cover stories

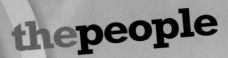

the**people**

the**moves**

the**talk**

BLUEBIRD POWDER DAY

As the white peaks get closer, my stomach tightens like a knotted rope. I've dreamed of my first heliboarding trip so many times. I've drooled over photos and videos of the rugged mountain range that soars from the ocean to higher than 13,000 feet (4,000 meters). I'm face-to-face with the steepest slope I've ever seen. I swallow hard and try to act cool, but my adrenaline levels are way off the charts!

The real deal

I am so excited to be part of this photo shoot. It's sunny, and the snow is fresh—a perfect bluebird powder day! Today's my big chance to prove that I'm the real deal—a professional rider who nails it when the pressure is on.

Awesome views

The helicopter touches down, and we scramble out with our gear. Suddenly, the wind settles down, and I'm awestruck by the view. Snow covers the landscape like a soft, white blanket. I hold my breath and hop off, landing with a POOF into deep, dry powder. The snow is so deep that it feels as if I'm free-falling with every turn as the snow flies in my face.

Paid to have fun

Approaching a rocky drop-off, I hear the helicopter's blades thundering near me. I know I'm being filmed, so I head for the highest point and bust a 360 (a full-circle trick) into bottomless space. I grab my board to keep my body compact as my white-and-blue world spins around me. I stomp the landing, laughing out loud. I can't believe I'm getting paid to have this much fun!

5

SNOW SPEAK

Don't get frozen out on the slopes. Stoke up on snowboard speak with the On the Radar guide!

backbowls
bowl-shaped slopes found behind the farthest peaks of a mountain resort

backcountry
areas that are not within the boundaries of a mountain resort

backside
a trick done with the rider's back facing the pipe wall or slope

banked turns
a snow feature with a nearly vertical slope that causes the rider's body to achieve a horizontal position as he or she carves through the turn

bindings
devices designed to hold a rider's boots to a snowboard

boxes
wide rectangular features, usually made of plastic, that are found in a terrain park

chutes
steep, narrow paths that require tight turns to ride down

cowboy stance
standing on a snowboard with knees bent; legs apart; and a tall, relaxed posture

detuned edges
edges of a freestyle board that have been dulled to prevent them from catching on boxes and rails

directional board
a freeride board with a wider nose than tail

drop-off
the point at which a slope becomes almost vertical

frontside
a trick done with the rider facing the pipe wall or slope

grabs
grabbing the edge of the board while airborne for extra stability and style points

halfpipe/pipe
a U-shaped feature carved out of snow built on a run steep enough to propel the rider into the air

heel/toe edges
the edge of the snowboard closest to the heels/toes of a strapped-in rider

kicker
a large jump that kicks you into the air

parallel GS
a giant slalom race that pits two competitors side by side on identical courses

powder
soft, dry snow that is freshly fallen and a pleasure to ride

quarterpipe
a snow feature with just one wall of a halfpipe

rail jam
a judged competition on a series of rails

regular stance
riding with the left leg in front

rotation
the amount of spinning involved in a trick

Skier X
a boardercross event at the X Games

slopestyle
a judged competition held in a terrain park that includes big kickers, rails, and other freestyle features

Snowboarder X
a boardercross event featured at the X Games

snow dome
an indoor riding and skiing facility

steeze
displaying class, style, and ease

stomp
to land a trick solidly

tabletop jump
a jump designed with a takeoff on one end, a flat top, and a sloped landing on the other

terrain parks
areas within a mountain resort that have freestyle features such as jumps, rails, and halfpipes

360
a freestyle trick that involves a full-circle rotation

tweaking out
stretching out a move to its fullest extension

GLOSSARY

adrenaline
a hormone found in the human body that causes the heart to beat faster

amplitude
the height that a rider achieves while performing an aerial trick

consecutive
one after the other

Grand Prix
the longest-running snowboard competition tour in the United States

incidental contact
elbowing or collisions that happen between competitors that are unintentional

physical therapy
the medical treatment of someone with a muscular injury

prestigious
held in high esteem; very well regarded

sponsors
businesses that financially support talented riders

BOARDING TO WIN

After the invention of the first modern snowboard in the late 1970s, riders started to compete against one another to be the fastest, highest boarder. As equipment improved, moves were pushed to the limit and competitions became big crowd-pullers.

Suicide Six

The first National Snowboard Championships took place in 1982 at Suicide Six, a small ski resort in Vermont. The event consisted of a steep, downhill race. Some racers were timed at more than 60 miles (96 kilometers) per hour. The contest evolved into the U.S. Open Snowboarding Championships, one of the sport's most prestigious events, with prizes totaling $250,000.

The halfpipe is born

In 1983 Tom Sims organized the first halfpipe contest at Soda Springs near Lake Tahoe, California, on the world's first man-made pipe. In 1985 Breckenridge Ski Resort in Colorado built a pipe with 5-foot (1.5 m) walls for the Snowboarding World Championships. After the contest, the pipe became a permanent feature on which riders could practice. By 1988 every major resort was scrambling to make its own pipe. During the early 1990s, the snowboarding craze had swept Europe and European countries began hosting world championships.

Jake Burton was one of the first snowboarders to take to the slopes. The skier-turned-snowboarder is also the founder of Burton Snowboards, a leading U.S. snowboard manufacturer and pro snowboarding sponsor.

X Games rock!

The first Winter X Games were held in 1997 at Big Bear Lake, California. The event was aired on TV, giving many people their first real taste of extreme snowboarding. In 2002 the Games moved to Aspen, Colorado, where they have remained. In 2008 X Games XII saw a 33 percent increase in TV viewers from the year before and the International Olympic Committee (IOC) began looking at X Games events such as slopestyle to add to the Olympic lineup.

Part of the U.S. Olympic snowboarding team poses in 2010. Five of the members—including Hannah Teter *(third from left)* and Shaun White *(far right)*—won medals.

Olympic glory

Snowboarding first appeared at the 1998 Winter Olympics in Nagano, Japan. Halfpipe and giant slalom (GS) were the featured events, and snowboard cross (or X) was added to the list at the 2006 Games. Slopestyle will debut at the 2014 Olympics in Sochi, Russia.

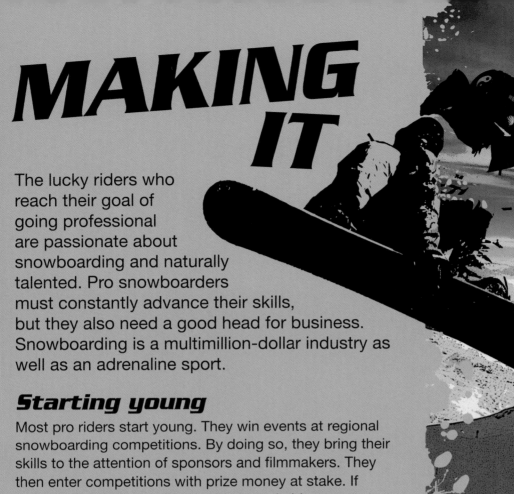

MAKING IT

The lucky riders who reach their goal of going professional are passionate about snowboarding and naturally talented. Pro snowboarders must constantly advance their skills, but they also need a good head for business. Snowboarding is a multimillion-dollar industry as well as an adrenaline sport.

Starting young

Most pro riders start young. They win events at regional snowboarding competitions. By doing so, they bring their skills to the attention of sponsors and filmmakers. They then enter competitions with prize money at stake. If successful, they are invited to compete in bigger events.

Ticket to ride

Living within a reasonable distance of a mountain resort and buying a season pass are bare necessities to budding professional snowboarders. To make it as a pro, they must spend as many hours of the day as possible making turns and launching off kickers. To fund their dream, some snowboarders teach snowboarding or take night jobs so that they are free to ride all day.

Riders on film

Some snowboarders are given small parts in snowboarding movies that highlight the glory of a professional rider's lifestyle. The movies show them jetting all over the world to enjoy deep powder turns. Few videos show the hours spent traveling, meeting with the press and sponsors, climbing the pipe over and over to nail a trick, or sitting in a hotel waiting for the weather to clear.

WINNING IT!

A parallel GS (PGS) event features two riders who race simultaneously on identical courses.

Incidental contact is allowed in a boardercross race, but intentional pushing, elbowing, or grabbing is not.

Professional riders can choose from several different disciplines within the sport of snowboarding. Few riders can master them all, so for competitions, they specialize in the events at which they excel. These are some of the most popular snowboarding events.

Boardercross (BX)

Four to six competitors race in the boardercross event. They compete over a course that can include big kickers, banked turns, and bumps. The first rider to cross the finish line wins. Staying ahead of the pack helps a rider avoid collisions, especially as incidental contact is allowed during the event. To complete jumps as quickly as possible, BX racers keep their bodies and boards close to the snow.

Giant slalom

GS is a timed race around gates. To achieve the fastest time, riders explode out of their starting positions and turn above each gate. This reduces skidding and helps the rider gain a more direct line downhill. The closer to the gates riders dare to turn, the faster their times.

Slopestyle and halfpipe

Slope and pipe are contests of difficulty, amplitude, and steeze. The height and number of rotations of tricks are vital to earning a high score, but tweaking out each move and grab to its fullest will also impress the judges. The more tricks a rider can cram into each run, the better. A rider's final score is the best of two runs.

Competitors try to lay down a solid first run on the halfpipe. Then they try more difficult tricks on the second run to improve their score.

DRESS FOR SUCCESS

Each type of snowboarding competition requires its own equipment, which is specially designed to help a rider win. Serious riders know that the right board, boots, bindings, and clothes make a huge difference, and they never compete without a helmet.

boardercross padded sweater

Boardercross

Most BX riders use a stiff board specially designed for BX. BX can be very fast, and there is contact between riders. Competitors wear a lot of body protection, including padded shorts and sweaters, both equipped with jointed, hard-plastic protectors. A full-face helmet and a mouth guard are used to protect the face and teeth.

hardboot

Giant Slalom

GS competitors wear hardboots (similar to ski boots but made especially for snowboarding) and plate bindings (step-in bindings that fit hardboots). They also use a GS alpine board. This narrow, long board has an aggressive sidecut made specifically for powerful, fast turns and stability at high speeds.

Slopestyle

Most slope riders wear padded shorts under their pants. They use a twin-tip board with edges adjusted so they won't catch on the rail slides.

padded shorts

twin-tip board

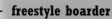

freestyle boarder

Superpipe

To rock the pipe, riders wear lightweight pipe gloves with bright graphics. These emphasize their grabs and make the judges notice them. They ride freestyle boards with sharp edges to carve up the icy walls of halfpipes. Padded shorts under pants are a good idea for extra protection when learning a new trick.

SHAUN WHITE

THE STATS

Name: Shaun White
Date of birth: September 3, 1986
Hometown: Carlsbad, California
Home mountain: Park City, Utah
Job: Professional snowboarder and skateboarder

Sponsored at seven

Before he was a year old, Shaun White had had heart surgery twice. But his heart condition never stopped him from joining in the fun on family skiing vacations. His older brother taught him to snowboard, and by the time he was seven, Shaun was offered a sponsorship by Burton Snowboards. A couple of years later, he met skateboarding legend, Tony Hawk, who took him under his wing in the skateboarding world.

Olympic gold

While training for the 2010 Winter Olympics, Shaun perfected his new trick called the Tomahawk. This was two diagonal rotations with a blind landing (where he couldn't see the landing before his board hit the snow). He traveled to his own backcountry training facility by snowmobile or helicopter. These secret training sessions, nicknamed Project X, proved to be a success, as Shaun stomped the Tomahawk and won his second consecutive Olympic superpipe gold medal.

Teen star

While Shaun grew in inches and mastered some impressive tricks, he swept five consecutive U.S. national overall snowboarding titles. At the age of 13, he began competing at a professional level. Shaun won his first Olympic gold in 2006, at the Torino, Italy, games. He became the first athlete to win four consecutive gold medals at the Winter X Games from 2007 to 2010. He was also first to win gold medals at both Winter and Summer X Games in 2007 and 2011.

On top of the game

Shaun White is considered the most recognized and financially successful rider of his generation, with starring roles in multiple video games and snowboarding movies. His career continues to pick up momentum with appearances in TV ads for his sponsors. He uses the competitive pressure from other top riders to push himself to constantly progress and learn new tricks. He plans to take part in the 2014 Winter Olympics in Sochi, Russia.

KIM KRAHULEC

On the Radar spends a week with BX specialist Kim Krahulec, as she prepares for the Chevy U.S. Snowboarding Grand Prix competition.

blog   **news**   **events**

SUNDAY

I rode the boardercross course at Copper Mountain, Colorado, really working on my starts. I finally nailed some good ones. My gym workout was light today. I did two hours of weight training with some stretching. My knee's been swollen, so I'm hoping it will heal in time for the Grand Prix later this week.

MONDAY

I tuned and waxed my boards and packed my bag for Boreal, California. I went to physical therapy because my knee is still swollen and aching.

TUESDAY

I got up at 4 A.M. to make my 7 A.M. flight to Reno, Nevada. I slept in the team van all the way up to Boreal. The house we are staying in is sweet! I went to the hill to register and check out the course.

blog   news   events

WEDNESDAY

I slept until 8 A.M. I inspected the course in detail and took a couple of training runs. My knee really ached, and it kept me from riding my best. It was so frustrating! I wrapped it in ice after I trained, hoping that would help it heal before the big event tomorrow.

THURSDAY

Race day. My knee still really hurts, but I decided to race regardless. I had to fight through the semifinal heat, but I made it to the finals! The final heat was a tough one. I had a bad start and got tangled up with one of my closest friends. I was still able to somehow take third place and win $3,000—not bad for a day of riding! We packed up the van right after the race and headed home. It had been a long day, and I was tired.

FRIDAY

We finally arrived back home at 2 A.M. I collapsed into bed!

SATURDAY

Our coach seemed to have no sympathy for us! We spent three hours working sooo hard in the gym today, and then I headed to physical therapy to check out my knee again. It's been a crazy week, but nailing that tough BX course and winning solid cash to pay my bills has made it all worthwhile!

ON THE MAP

A snowboarder kills it on the halfpipe at the X Games in Colorado *(left)*. Steep, deep, and rad, Verbier, Switzerland *(below)*, is a favorite destination for photo shoots.

With tons of talent and luck, a professional rider could be invited to film a video or compete anywhere in the world. Here are some of the places to see top riders in action.

Aspen, Colorado

Aspen, Colorado, hosts the X Games. Its dramatic, snow-covered peaks make it one of the best sites in the world. Here, tens of thousands of spectators gather daily during the last weekend of January for a free, up-close view of the world's top winter sport celebrities. Snowboarder X, Skier X, Snowmobile Big Air, slopestyle, and superpipe are just some of the sports to see.

Verbier, Switzerland

Home to the Verbier Xtreme, Verbier hosts the granddaddy of big-mountain snowboard competitions. Founded in 1996, the Verbier Xtreme is held on the Bec des Rosses—a steep, sheer face that is 1,960 feet (597 m) high! The contest has grown into an international Freeride World Tour, with four qualifying events around the world and the grand finale at Verbier.

Valdez, Alaska *(below left)*, is one of the most remote and challenging snowboarding locations in the world. Banff, Canada *(below right)*, has some of the best snowboarding runs in Canada.

Valdez, Alaska

Founded in 1993, the King of the Hill and Queen of the Hill contests put Valdez snowboarding on the map. They are part of the Tailgate Alaska World Freeride Festival, a rider-judged, big-mountain contest. Set on nearly 4,000 feet (1,219 m) of powder-wrapped vertical, the king and queen of this hill must land huge airs and have nerves of steel. Valdez is also a popular destination for filming snowboarding movies because of its endless steep chutes and spectacular scenery.

Banff, Canada

Some professional snowboarders are not cut out for televised contests and all the hassles of being a snowboarding star. They love their sport but want to stay out of the limelight. These snowboarders often head to Banff, in Alberta, Canada, which has some of the cleanest snow in the world. Here, pro snowboarders can ride some of the most remote, untouched powder on the planet as their daily job. These boarders choose to be a guide with a helicopter or snowcat tour company. They oversee tours for vacationers and in their free time shred the Canadian Rockies to the max!

CELIA MILLER

Well established as a snowboarding film star, Celia Miller has set her sights on making the U.S. slopestyle team for the 2014 Winter Olympics. On the Radar asks Celia what it takes to be a pro snowboarder.

How did you get into snowboarding?

When I was 16, my mother told me I needed to get a job, so I started selling lift tickets at my local resort. I made friends with snowboarders, and they got me to try it.

What is your most memorable backcountry filming experience?

Every backcountry trip is an experience whether it's good or bad. I have ridden with some amazing people and had some of the best days snowboarding in my life on those trips. It's a feeling that's hard to describe, so I will keep those moments to myself!

Which riders do you admire and why?

I have a ton of respect for the older generation of snowboarders who are still killing it, like Jeremy Jones, Peter Line, Chad Otterstrom, Terje Håkonsen, and Janna Meyen-Weatherby. I think many of the younger generation of snowboarders take for granted what is available to them today.

How are backcountry skills and slopestyle skills connected?

Riding the terrain park really helps me with my core tricks. Then, when I take it to the backcountry, I feel confident. I do tend to perfect more new tricks in the backcountry, however. The powder there is a lot softer to land on than terrain parks.

Do you have any strategies or tips for winning?

I pick a run and stick to what I know I can do. It sounds simple, but when I'm in a contest and feeling pressure, it's easy to get intimidated and distracted watching other riders.

What tricks are you currently working on?

Double and triple flips are all the rage. I have been trying a few in the backcountry. I feel comfortable going upside down, so I am trying to use that to my advantage.

What are the two coolest places you've ever ridden?

Jackson Hole, Wyoming—it's a huge mountain with steep, diverse terrain. And Chamonix, France. This can be a very dangerous place, but the freeriding there is probably some of the best in the world.

THE BACKFLIP

1

2

The aerial backflip is a spectacular and challenging move. Before advancing to a backflip, the rider should be able to perform confident backflips on a trampoline and solid takeoffs, grabs, and landings on all jumps. He or she should also have mastered 360-degree rotations.

Why do it?

The backflip is an essential trick for a boarder to master. It is a basic move that allows boarders to progress to more advanced moves including many halfpipe tricks. Mastering the backflip not only helps competitors add to their bag of difficult tricks, but it also helps a rider learn aerial awareness and safety.

Essential technique

- Focus on the lift at takeoff.
- Achieve height to perform the rotation.
- Pinpoint the landing site at the highest point of the jump.

3

HOW IT'S DONE

1. The rider chooses a medium-size jump and focuses on gaining lift at the takeoff point.
2. The rider then brings the knees toward the body and curls into a tight ball of rotating energy.
3. Once the rider has rotated 90 degrees, the rider looks back for the landing point.
4. The rider lands with the weight centered over the board. The rider then bends the knees to absorb the impact on landing.

4

STOKED TO RIDE!

My story by Josh Ort

For my 11th birthday, my parents bought me a series of snowboarding lessons at a local snow dome. The instructor showed us the cowboy stance, the heel and toe edges, and how to zigzag down the slope. It was like learning a whole new language! On my first run, the air rushed past my face and shapes of people whooshed by. I saw my parents smiling at the bottom, and I felt so happy! From that second, all I wanted to do was snowboard.

After that, I built up my skills and confidence enough to join the Maverix Snow Camp Youth Development Team. Joining the squad really helped me to improve my skills. Then, I was lucky enough to be sponsored by Surfanic Clothing. They supplied me with a jacket, snow pants, goggles, and gloves for training and competitions.

I trained indoors twice a week at a snow dome near where I live. This meant that I could ride all year-round, then go on vacation to the mountains a couple of times a year. I also practiced on a trampoline after school with a training board, doing spins and grabs. Even when I wasn't snowboarding, I still wanted to be active—trying out new moves on my skateboard or practicing free running. I never sat still for long!

I loved learning new tricks and being creative! Plus, the element of danger gave me a sense of achievement when I conquered my fear of doing something. The hardest trick I have ever done is a 720 with a grab—that's two full rotations in the air! It's such a great feeling to land that!

I want to keep improving and perhaps one day compete in the Olympic Games. I'd love to have my own snowboard coaching company so I can teach other kids how to have as much fun as I do!

NAILIN' THE RAILS

Just as skateboarders slide on rails, snowboarders perform similar moves. Here are some of the tricks seen at rail competitions, known as rail jams.

Gap rail

A gap in a rail makes it necessary for a rider to jump from one section to the other, making the move more challenging and daring.

Rainbow rail

These rails are shaped in a curve like that of a rainbow. The first rainbow rails that snowboarders tried to slide were young trees that had bowed over in the woods. Rainbow rails can be found in terrain parks in different heights, widths, and variations.

Kinked rail

Kinked rails and boxes have a flat-down-flat section. This is a horizontal platform followed by an incline and then another flat section. Some kinked rails have several flat-down-flat sections in a row.

Frontside boardslide

During a boardslide, the snowboarder slides at an angle perpendicular to the rail. The term *frontside* was first used in surfing to describe a move that was carried out facing the wave. In the case of freestyle snowboarding, it means that the rider is facing uphill *toward* the slope or halfpipe wall.

This rider is jumping from one side of a gap rail and landing in a frontside boardslide down the other side—a difficult trick, if he makes it!

On a rainbow rail, the rider bends the knees to hug the arch of the rail, while riding with the board pointing toward the end of the rail.

This rider is boarding on a kinked rail and is preparing to slide into the dip of the flat-down-flat.

A frontside boardslide is performed on the tail of the board. It is important to stay centered and avoid catching the edge of the board on the rail.

KILLIN' IT!

Since the invention of snowboarding, records have been made and broken. But there are some that are so amazing, they may stand for decades to come.

Shred 'til you're dead!

Who: Donna Vano
When: Born in 1953
Where: South Lake Tahoe, California
What: Most national snowboarding titles
How: At the age of 40, Donna retired as a pro skier and swapped her skis for a snowboard. She is still competing and winning in GS, slalom, BX, slopestyle, and superpipe.

Shooting for perfect

Who: Shaun White
When: February 18, 2010
Where: 2010 Winter Olympics, Vancouver, Canada
What: Highest Olympic score in superpipe
How: Perfecting his new trick, the Tomahawk, Shaun scored 48.4 out of 50 on his final superpipe run, winning his second Olympic gold medal.

Unbelievable airtime

Who: Mads Jonsson
When: May 9, 2005
Where: Hemsedal, Norway
What: Longest tabletop jump—187 feet (57 m)
How: Jonsson performed this feat on a specially built tabletop jump in the backcountry. Its long, steep ramp allowed him to gain the speed he needed without a snowmobile.

Split-second speed

Who: Darren Powell
When: May 2, 1999
Where: Les Arcs, France
What: Highest speed on a snowboard—an incredible 125 miles (202 km) per hour
How: Using a specially designed speedsuit and helmet, Powell headed straight down a long, narrow, and extremely steep chute.

Loads of laps

Who: Tammy McMinn
When: April 20, 1998
Where: Atlin, British Columbia, Canada
What: Most vertical distance heliboarded within 24 hours—305,525 feet (93,124 m)
How: Tammy hired a personal trainer to help her build strength and endurance and rode an average of seven nonstop hours a day. This helped her to prepare for 101 laps on Paradise Peak, a mountain in the Coast Mountains. In total, she boarded 232.3 miles (374 km) in 14 hours and 50 minutes!

Hucking into space

Who: Terje Håkonsen
When: February 2007
Where: Oslo, Norway
What: Highest air
How: While qualifying for the Arctic Challenge in Oslo in 2007, he jumped 32 feet (9.8 m) off the quarterpipe with a backside 360.

Insane riding!

Who: Johan Olofsson (aka Johan O)
When: 1996
Where: Chugach Range, Alaska
What: Most challenging backcountry line
How: In the movie *TB5*, Johan O rode a straight line down Cauliflower Chutes (a slope of more than 40 degrees), traveling more than 3,000 feet (914 m) in 35 seconds and averaging nearly 50 miles (80 km) per hour.

GET MORE INFO

Books

Barr, Matt, and Chris Moran. *Snowboarding*. Minneapolis: Lerner Publications Company, 2004. Read this book to learn about the history, techniques, and superstars of the sport.

Doeden, Matt. *Shaun White*. Minneapolis: Lerner Publications Company, 2011. Learn about the exploits of one of the premier snowboarders and skateboarders of all time.

Figorito, Marcus. *Friction and Gravity: Snowboarding Science*. New York: Rosen Classroom, 2009. Learn all about the science of snowboarding, from carving down the mountain to performing gravity-defying tricks.

Rottman, Alexander, and Nici Pederzolli. *Freestyle Snowboarding: Tricks, Skills and Techniques*. Richmond Hill, ON: Firefly Books, 2010. Check out this book to learn—with the help of step-by-step photos—how snowboarding professionals perform over 60 different tricks!

Websites

Kids Health: Snowboarding Safety Tips
http://kidshealth.org/parent/firstaid_safe/outdoor/safety_snowboarding.html
Snowboarding can be dangerous. Learn how to keep safe on the slopes at this website.

LiveStrong: Snowboarding
http://www.livestrong.com/snowboarding/
The snowboarding page of the LiveStrong website offers important safety information.

Shaun White Official Website
http://www.shaunwhite.com/
Visit pro snowboarder Shaun White's official website to get up-to-date news, photos, and videos of the world-class athlete.

Shred Betties
http://www.shredbetties.com/
This snowboarding magazine focuses on girls and women who enjoy the sport.

INDEX